Forest Full of Rain

LALA KOEHN

Forest Full of Rain

1982
Sono Nis Press
Victoria, British Columbia

Canadian Cataloguing in Publication Data

Koehn, Lala, 1936-
Forest Full of Rain

Poems
ISBN 0-919462-95-2

I. Title
PS8571.03F6   C811'.54   C82-091082-1
PR9199.3.K62F6

The publication of this book would not have been possible
without the assistance of the Canada Council.

Published by
SONO NIS PRESS
1745 Blanshard Street
Victoria, British Columbia
Canada v8w 2j8

Designed, printed and bound in Canada by
MORRISS PRINTING COMPANY LTD.
Victoria, British Columbia

for those who will never grow old,
to whom fantasy and magic are real

Other poetry books by Lala Koehn

Portraits   1977

Sandpoems   1979

The Eyes of the Wind   1981

ACKNOWLEDGEMENTS

Some of the poems in this collection have appeared in the follow-
ing magazines: *Manitoba Writers News*, *Freelance*, *The Martlet*,
Dandelion, *The Malahat Review*, *Wot*. Several have been broad-
cast by the CBC in The Hornby Collection.

I am grateful to the editors and publishers concerned.

I also wish to thank my classmates at the University of Victoria
and the members of our small poetry group for all their help and
guidance, but most of all for their friendship and caring.

Contents

Prefatory Note

These poems were written during the years 1979 to 1981. The manuscript is divided into four sections. The first two sections, "The Caragana Roots" and "Do Not Open The Sea" deal with the sense of loss of what I think of as my second home for 20 years, Saskatchewan. On arriving in Victoria in 1977 I realized that I could not live in the past alone, and must turn my eyes away from "where the wheat is trees," and learn to see the cedar and the sea surrounding me. The third section, "You and I are Homeless," is one of love poems, of the reaching out to keep our hands warm. Reality and fantasy are one in the childlike world, where wooden horses eat pebbles, and silverspoons sail across the sea under snakeskin masts, if we only take the wings that are offered to us. The last section, "The Three," speaks of such a world.

I

CARAGANA ROOTS

Where the wheat is trees L.K.

BECAUSE SHE MUST

I will bring down the Northern Lights
to tear open the low sky. I will dig
up the hills here, cup the valley
in my hands like her breasts
and I will bring them to her
with the wisp of straw
that clung to her skin.
She loved me then,
she will love me now

AND BEYOND US WERE THE HILLS

You are lying! suddenly red, hot wires
stab my cheek, nestling against your beard,
igniting your eyes with rage.
*The bird nest I gave you when we met
remember, God damn it, all I ask
is honesty!* You push me away,
digging your hands into the desertlike
soil of the narrow ridge where we sit,
your fingers now talons of a huge bird,
taller then the darkening peaks
surrounding us. You carry the rusty dirt
to the edge of a sudden drop.

I can feel the hill slide from under
me. 'He will move this hill and I will
perish at the bottom of the canyon,
he will fly over me, cover my body with dirt.'
I came to be here, if only for a little while
I say, my eyes touching your hand, ready
to heave the hollowed dirt. You turn around,
no longer a bird, only a man. *Come,* you say
opening your hands, the dirt falling
through your fingers.

We descend the narrow path carved into
the hill, a sluggish stream reflects
the almost moon.
You open the gate of the barbed wire
fence with one, smooth sweep, close it
behind us.

IT WAS THAT KIND OF A SPRING

The meadowlark perches on the iron gate.
I must walk up to the other hills I tell him,
the hills that curve the horizon away
from fences and rivercourses;
where the hairy-stemmed crocuses grow,
and the wild strawberry leaf greens. You see,
my shadow has become useless
after all these years, and I must bury it
there, under the protection of a thorny
wild-rose bush
And the sun?
The sun I will ask to take a different course.

THE ABANDONED GOSLING

Is it the spring, finally in June,
you want to ride the river downstream,
bobbing up and down, for miles and miles
the wind blowing in the same direction?

Is it the wings you want to use,
to try to fly back, from where you had begun,
then try again, to ride downstream,
this time perhaps, against the wind?

I trace your efforts on a piece of paper,
draw charts of treacherous places
of the rivercourse, the sudden bends,
twisted roots of dead trees, the undercurrents
you might encounter, but I forgot, you have
not yet learned how to read, down only
covering your body.

I could put a spell upon you,
charm your down away; I could lend you
my wings, but they are naked. My pinfeathers
were plucked one by one, I can use them
only to map out your danger,
and I cannot remember the chant.

THE LETTER IN SPRING

You tell me about the baby bush-rabbit
under your door steps, nibbling on the grass:
it is so little, it would fit into your palm.
And that you and I are shedding our skins
like snakes, soon we will be us again.
I am trying to recall your door steps,
how little is a baby rabbit,
how green is grass,
what does one do with discarded skins
could they fit into my palm?

LE FORUM AU PARADIS

for Monique Valdeneige

There is this happy-pink brick
house (or is it a church, I cannot
tell, just flying over) surrounded
by all kinds of lollipop flowers,
trees, formally trimmed, with chocolate
dipped raisins, dotted all over with
sugar-starched doilies.
In the middle of that lush growth is
a courtyard closed in by a high (even
higher than that) wall, paved by grey
stones like sad eyes. Inside it are
people who are very small. They look
like coloured pin-heads, (perhaps
because each one of them is wearing
a different-hued hat, though I can't
be sure). But I am sure they are
thinking the same kind of thoughts:
How do we get out from here to see,
whether the happy-pink bricks are
a house or a church? Also — does
the stuff surrounding it taste as
yummy as it smells?

I do sympathize with them, flying over.
I know how it feels to be the size
of a pin and not able to climb over
a high, (even higher than that) wall.

THE CARAGANA ROOTS

for Terrence Heath

You come, prairie wind on your heels,
the vast sky, curiously distant, curiously
close, still in your eyes. You hold me
for a moment, then let go, walk away
toward the garden.

"All this was nothing but rock" I point
to the profusion of flowers, the shrubs
whose name I still do not know. You look
at the three ancient cedars, your eyes
sweeping over the naked dark trunks,
their plumed crowns still strong, still
reaching out. *"They are very, very old"*
I explain apologetically, embarrassed
that anything could be so old. (It is
always like this; they come, bringing
the smell of my home, where the wheat is
trees,) *"how anything would want to live
for so long!"* you say.

*"Look at the welts in the grass; how they
fan out, disappear under the house.
They are the cedar's roots."* You are perched
on a huge boulder, breathing in the sea,
*"I suppose that's what keeps them green,
holding the four walls together!"* Your
staccato laugh bounces through the air;
you jump off, walk through the rose arbour,
("they are so damn pretentious!") down the steps,
to the cove. You pick kelp off the tide-
exposed shore, shake it like green snakes
with bulbous heads, ignoring the huge arm
of the breakwater. *"What are the yellow bushes
growing on the rocks?"* you call, *"Spanish broom."*
You run back up, stand beside me. *"It's caragana
with a fancy name; the blossoms are just
jazzier,"* you say with a poker face.
I pick one of the flowers.

Later, I show you a bird nest, stuck above
my kitchen door, downy feathers, bits of
whitewash strewn over the back steps.
A bird with sun-bleached brick-red breast
sits undisturbed beside it.
*"I guess you are like the caragana roots
that followed you here, and have settled
in spite of it all,"* you say, your eyes
on me, far away. I look at you, the tiny
yellow flower still in my hand; suddenly
I feel I am at home.

THE BACKROOM HOUSE

for Valentine

In the backroom of his house
mediaeval ladies with elongated
eyes and faces weave their static
veils through his dreams cut to
miniatures.
I am a guest in his frontroom,
where he hung misty landscapes
of fields covered with snow,
narrow sloughs, stretched and spiked
on naked bushes.
Here you must feel at home he tells me.
We argue; whether the patches
on the horizon of pale-yellow
and green turning into grey,
are a vision of an artist or
the dying light caught and broken
by a crystal prism

THE EAGLE NEST CLIFF

High above the sea
there is a deserted eagle nest,
it turned into a cliff, waiting
for the bird's return.

The eagle, before he left, gave me
his three feathers to remember him by
and said: "This is a safe place,
wait for me, I will be back."

The grass has grown tall 7 times 7
since then. The sea is washing
the rock away   soon
it will swallow the sky.
I am still holding his feathers,
listening for the sound of his wings.
It is almost wintertime.

II

DO NOT OPEN THE SEA

The wall is now higher than the roof of my house <small>L.K.</small>

ON MY BEDSIDE TABLE

Daffodils, hyacinths a twig
of cherry blossoms; I have not
replaced the flowers for many days
now. They are still in my white vase,
their droopy heads hanging over
the rim. It is not easy to smell
the spring with someone beside you
who is not there.

THE BOWL
THAT MOLDS THE ISLAND

The sky sits low today,
a bowl of milky glass turned
over the island, the fallen leaves
the yellowing grass.
I pick the tallest dry hollyhock
stalk, and I try to lift up the bowl
to see where the light comes from,
what makes it almost translucent.
I poke and prod at the rim,
molded tightly into the ground;
it falls, breaks the hollyhock
in half. I try again.
The edge of the bowl is now jagged,
cuts the stalk into small pieces,
the bowl sinks lower, lower,
my head touches the bottom;
I crouch, brace myself to lift it
up once more. My fingertips push
through the glass, there is no feeling
in my fingers, red trickles
through the cracks,
it must be the sun
it must be
the sun

A HAWKER OF TRANSPARENT THINGS

each morning the sun
explodes another riddle of
the night just passed
    I bend over the burned soil
    collecting the fragments
    with a misers hand to fill my jug

the jug lies broken
at the bottom of a dry riverbed
shattered by silence
into a thousand pieces
the smell of chalk
of husked scorched seeds hangs
in the pale heat of sky
    I pick a handful of dust   mix it
    with sweat from my feet
    piece by piece
    I mend the jug   making it whole

I squeeze 3 stones
will the water wash
each splinter transparent   the jug is full now
brimming over with moon-round
looking-glass images
I set my wares upon my head
my day begins

THE WILL-NOT-BE-EMPTY NEST

If I could trust the eveness of my fingers
and to be careful of the season,
I would pry loose this useless nest
from the tree that bears no fruit.
But each time I stretch my hand to bring the nest
down, a many-beaked sinewy neck darts over the edge,
rakes my fingers bloody.
"Be still" I tell my hands, clawing my belly,
"be careful for another season".

Sometime, not that long ago.

Mother,

Do you remember the gold coloured handkerchief, with the tatted lace, you gave me when I was growing up? "It is your turn for fancy things" you said, putting a plain, white linen one into your bodice. I bring it with me now, coming home to show you, that I have taken good care of it all these years.

I saw you walking ahead of me, through the park, passed the purple chrysanthemum beds, (you still don't know, that each spring I steal the yellow and red tulips that grow there, to make a bouquet for you, for Mother's Day) walking tall and straight like a queen. Your white, silk turban pinned with the cameo brooch covering your black hair. And I saw passers-by turn around after you with pleasure. No one noticed the little girl with the matchstick legs, and the giant, blue ribbon in the thin blond hair, walking behind you. "This is my mother!" I wanted to shout, proud to have a mother as beautiful as you.

You went into the "Morskie Oko" Coffee House, with the glassed-in verandah, to meet your friends for "Fife," to sit and listen to the orchestra, to sip "half-a-black." I hid inside a doorway, saw you getting up to dance, the dance floor turning around and around. By suppertime, you were saying good-bye to your friends, walking away quickly, heading for home. I followed you, as fast as I could, trying to catch up, as you were turning into the narrow walk. But you disappeared inside a large, ugly plaster-peeling house, with broken steps and balustrades. I ran through the garden to look in the window and saw you sitting by your little polished table, amongst your lovely cushions strewn all over the floor, all the kilims, paintings, calmly reading a letter. I ran back to the front door, through the hall, knocking hard at your door and called loudly: "Mother, let me in, let me in I must show you the lace handkerchief!" An old woman appeared in the door crack and said: "Your Mother is dead, buried in Canada a long time ago. Go home, and show it to her there!" Mother, I do not dare, I have spilled ink all over it.

28

THE WAITING

There is this tunnel under my other house.
My mother, my father disappeared inside it,
never came back. One thin streak of blood
seeped out, following me. The winding road
I took trying to escape it, twisted into a rope
as I stepped across this threshold. It bound my feet.

My children, curious, went back to the tunnel
to look, and now are bringing me pails and pails
of sand, coming up to rest their eyes. I have not
ventured near it, the rope around my feet
will not permit.

I try to adjust. Kindly, and with a smile
I accept the sand my children heap around
my curved reclining chair. I wiggle my toes
in it. It feels good, and I tell them that, (they
are so easily disappointed.)
The other day I asked them for seeds. Nothing much,
maybe marigolds, double daisics. They said they could
not find them, but they would try. And this is more
than I can expect.

Sometimes I wish the tunnel would collapse,
afraid rats might be breeding in it.
I do not like to think that this is the place
where my mother and father are trying to rest.
I also worry about my children.
The room I am forced to recline in is sunny,
and I am less afraid. I can hear the flies buzzing,
and I am grateful.

THE OTHER WOMAN'S HOUSE

The house I have moved in
is a kind woman's house. None
of the rooms remind me of my other
one. It must have taken a great
deal of thought on her part. (Even
the baking she had left from last
Christmas on the top kitchen shelf
looks smaller and daintier
than I used to make.)

Every so often I go into the family
room to find the best place for
my flowerpots. I am not familiar
with the sunny side. Except that every
corner is taken by her family's
rhythmic clatter of needles, knitting
yards and yards of woolly mufflers.
I do not like to disturb the pattern.
Quietly I leave my plants in the middle
of the room, close the door behind me
carefully. I lose directions, enter
the wrong hall, the wrong room, push
my furniture in and out, to arrange it
later.

The faucet in the laundry room sounds
familiar, the dripping steady and
measured. I mesh my hands under it;
the drops look the same as the ones
I remember from my other house,
I feel welcome.

The sound of a piano drifts from
the attic. I tiptoe up, over every
third broken step, stand in the shade
of the rafters, to see who is playing.
There is a woman sitting there, spinning
on the round piano stool, striking
a chord each time she faces the keyboard.
It sounds so familiar. I take off my shoes,
(I must not disturb her) and in my bare
feet, avoiding the nails in the floor,
I come closer, touch her shoulders,
as her hands are up to strike another
chord. "I would be thankful if you would
help me to remember the tune."
She turns around, looks at me briefly,
her eyes are the same shape as mine,
she is wearing my rings. "I too cannot
remember."

THERE ARE ALSO MY CHILDREN
WHO VISIT ME

Lately my children seem to be
disturbed. They knock at my door,
enter, without being asked to
come in.

> *You all seem to be in distress*
I tell them,
> > *Your knuckles seem to be whiter*
> > *than what I remember from your*
> > *last visit with me. I am glad*
> > *to see you, though I wish you would*
> > *come in, one at a time.*
> > *I have only one chair in my room,*
> > *and I do want to make you feel*
> > *comfortable.*
> > *"Mother, you make me feel unwanted"*
my oldest son says, his eyes shutting
the other children out into the hallway.

> > *Do sit down please on this petit*
> > *point chair, (I never did get around*
> > *to embroidering the other ones)*
> > *you have grown so tall, and my neck*
> > *gets tired looking up at you. I sit*
> > *on it Sundays, at dusk, for an hour*
> > *or so. It helps me to think about*
> > *the week that just passed."*
> > *"Mother, you are not listening"*

my son interrupts, glancing around
nervously, cracking his knuckles.

> *Could you wait for a moment,*
> *I must first close the windows.*
> *While you are waiting, do look*
> *at the photographs in the family*
> *album that I have collected of*
> *your three brothers and sister,*
> *which were taken when you all*
> *were quite little. On the last*
> *few pages you will find some*
> *of me, feeding your pets. The three*
> *cats, the snake that ate your canary,*
> *the dyed-pink chicken; the white*
> *mouse and her twelve babies, that*
> *looked like shrimp, (I helped to*
> *deliver them on the front steps,*
> *while peeling potatoes, remember?)*
> *O yes, there are quite a few of Muffi,*
> *your dog, who is still with me,*
> *now that he is blind.*

WIGILIA, GATHER AROUND ME
WHEN THE FIRST STAR APPEARS

The vases in my house stand empty.
In the corner of the yard grows
a huge holly tree. His mate,
much smaller, standing by the gate
bore but few berries this year.
Perhaps because it is that kind
of a year, perhaps she is timid
of his size.

For the last two days I have been selecting
the least conspicuous spot where
the branches can be cut, and she
still look intact. I count
the berries, divide them carefully
in my head, jotting down the numbers
by prickling my fingertips with
the sharp pointed leaves. I do not
want to be unjust to the tree
or myself. I choose three branches,
bring them into the house, but it's
not enough. There are too many vases
to be filled, other tasks still
awaiting me.

The table cloth from last year
shrunk, the table became even
smaller to accommodate all the
family, my real and adopted one;
a place must be set for an
absent member. I also worry
about the blue-flowered pattern
of the cloth. It is not right
for the occasion. I must be
white linen. It is Wigilia,
the traditional twelve-course
Christmas Eve meal. I count
the flowers painted on the cloth,
write down the number on
the steamy windowpanes; I pick
up the scissors to cut them out.
But there are too many of the blue
blossoms. And what's to be done
with the straw that must be placed
underneath? It will poke through
the holes.

> *Pull the shades down. I don't*
> *want anyone to see me wanting to*
> *make love to my wife.*
the father of my children says,
> *it's been a long time since we*
> *had any privacy. You been busy*
> *filling vases, counting berries,*
> *counting flowers. When will you*
> *have time for me?*
he asks, standing middle of the room,
his arms slack by his side, his fingers
twitching nervously, touching the pockets
of his grey trousers.

None of the blinds work;
The strings broke, I think, last
time ago. Perhaps when it gets
                    dark.
I turn around, look through
the jotted-down numbers on
the windows at the bright sunny sky.
            You will then gather the family
            and look for the first star
            to appear. I think, I will take
            a long walk, the dog needs exercise
he says. The gate scrapes the gravel
path, the dog's barking grows fainter.

I stand in the empty room, pick up
the vases, the copper glitters
in the sun.
            If I slice the three branches
            in half, it will fill six vases;
            one person less, will make
            the table seem bigger
I count in my head, picking up the knife.

DO NOT OPEN THE SEA INTO MY HOUSE

The salt from the earth is good and right,
but the salt from the waters will destroy
the whitewash on my house I tell the men
What must be done   must be done they sing,
carry the rock upon their shoulders to break the water;
their torn flesh mingles with ragged clothes.

When you are done, I shall greet you on my threshold
with bread and salt on a wooden tray. I will deck it
with white linen, bleached in the sun; but first my good men,
I must tend to your wounds. I tear the cloth,
to hold in place the healing power of the green bay leaves.
What must be done   must be done the men sing
as they carry the rock to break the water.

The wall is now higher than the roof of my house.
Nothing is left of the mountains.
We have taken care of it, woman the men say,
they tear off the cloth, stained with dried-on-flesh
give it back to me.
My good men, I bid you welcome with bread and salt
dark shadows crowding into my door,
Woman, we cannot stay. There is no sun here to bleach the linen,
your tray is bare

THE BED

There is no quiet in a bed grown too large.
The sheets, the colour of
wane, thin ghosts chatter with cold
their teeth,
the dreams rattle in sleep
their pallid bones.
There is no quiet in a feather
bed
the plucking   the plucking
goes on   and on
There is no quiet in a bed grown too large.
The only quiet sound
is the buzz of a fly,
waking at dawn

THE RUST-RED GROWN BEDS

(Cynghanedd)

Autumn leaves falling, autumn loves failing,
the green beds of old are the grown buds fled.
A rainy tree, long strands of rain trailing,
a wish, a word, a cry: Wash away red!

THE WALL I RAISED
IS OF THE FINEST MUSLIN

Breathe lightly. The wall I raised
between you and me is fragile.
It wavers, tips dangerously
with the slightest of movements. Do not speak
in your dreams, the wall might tumble.

> *Behind our closed lips and eyes*
> *lie the answers. Read our silences.*

I curved the wall and fluted
its edge with practiced fingers,
(it feels silken now, smooth from touch)
but when asleep, I always fear
it is stone, and it will bury me.

> *The weight of our word can crush a rock*
> *teach our fingers the art of touching.*

Each day I weigh your words in my hands
watch carefully the scale tip; the red
needle, like a long, bony finger,
moves, fluctuates between my eyes.
Its closeness has made me myopic. My
left arm jerks above my head, it stays up
will not come down. I try to lift the other,
its weight is pulling me, pulling me
down. If only you threw in a feather.

> *The damask quilt you bought*
> *to envelop us in warmth, is no more.*
> *last night, the geese came, claimed the down.*

THE VERDICT

Weep not for me my lover.
I have sold the better me
for considerable profit,
to be a respectable woman
in the eyes of all judges.

Now I stand before me
with my head bowed:
I am an adultress
in my own marriage bed.

AND MY SHRUBS WILL TAKE NEW ROOTS

Each day I perform ablutions,
wash away the caked-on crust;
the day cracks like a jigsaw-puzzle
sunburned soil.
And I watch the water become muddy and grey;
silt collects in my green, plastic pail;
I carry it outside to water my flowering
shrubs by the fence.

>*It is a good day for the sun* says the man,
>as he watches the water seep into the soil.
>*These shrubs are dying,*
>*but the flowers in the rockgarden*
>*are full of new buds, starting to blossom* he says

>*then we must destroy the fence,*
>*and give new food to the roots*   I tell him

Huge bolders are the fence in my backyard.
Now I sit here, splitting and cracking rocks
against one another, smoothing jagged edges,
my hands sunburned and freckled,
(I like to think they are freckles,
not brown spots of an ageing skin) soon
I will be done, and I will spread the fragments
where the fence used to be.
My shrubs will take new roots,
and there will be no need for me to labour,
to carry in the sun
the heavy pails of water

THE LANGUAGE OF FLOWERS

Long before,
he gave her a mug with painted-on
flowers. "These will last" he said.
It saddened her. She knew then
there would be only that one mug
on the table standing by an empty vase.

III

YOU AND I ARE HOMELESS

We must warm our hands L.K.

you are nearly as close
as you are far away
you lean over
your mouth upon mine
'I do not even know your name' I want to say
but your lips insistent
press my words inwards
and they clatter
down
my throat
   tiny
 hard
  pebbles
      shapes
I cannot distinguish
and I do not care
and it does not matter

MY LOVER MADE MY FINGER WHOLE

for M.

a red coat bleeds into the rain
wet moss   its crimson
ties rivuletting
        down the night
        dark hill   toward a stunned pale lake
        that lies
still   like a numb hand   with spread-out stumps
luminous fingers

I taste the bitter fragrance of a blueberry
leaf   touching my mouth
tiny leaves drip
raindrops on my eyelids
run down
        my cheeks
it is the rain
          it is
            the rain

I open my eyes   the moon tears
the clouds apart
the lake shivers
the trees are whole
a silver band slips upon my finger
my lover made my finger whole

THE BRUSH THAT PAINTED
THE HAIR BLACK

for M.

You hand me my scarf, saying:
"it smells of tobacco, of earth,
it smells of you.
Last time, before you left
I wanted to ask you for it,
to keep it while you were gone
but I did not dare".

At your feet there is a coiled body
of a nude woman,
burying her hands in black, angry hair;
her skin is aflame with red and amber
from a fire that I cannot see.
"Who is she?"   I want to ask
but I do not dare

ANOTHER YEAR,
ANOTHER TIME

A gutted-out cedar
mars the sky
    scarred arms shred its cloth
    torn by cold
    lightening

tattered rags too thin

I ask two crows above
to spread their wings
to keep us warm

THE BRUSH THAT
TOUCHES YOUR CANVAS

The sea surges, rising wildly,
hurling swirls of steel-blue
cavernous eyes into the black holes
of a blind rock. White froth splashes
my face, salt bites my eyelids,
my lips.
Why are your skies green,
the colour of meadows on soft, rainy days,
but your sea is so angry? I ask,
wiping my face;
this is a selfportrait you say,
touching briefly my hair with a gentle hand

BUT I CANNOT SHOW YOU THE PLACE

let me tell you how clear the sky is,
how a star wants to journey
from one to another star,
how the lights on the other shore blink
blink   warning about falling;
the place is called The Lapping Waters Point

but I cannot show you the place;
its cliffs jut out above the sea,
the path which leads to it,
elbowed between sharply descending dense growth,
closes behind me in a tangle
of arbutus and other strange trees
and I sit here   on the yellow dry grass
listening to the waves   lapping
washing under the cliff   and I cannot tell you
what arms are trying to comfort me
whose hands are saying:
"you are a virgin who bore many children
your sky is studded with satellites"

YOU AND I ARE HOMELESS
WITH A ROOF ABOVE OUR HEADS

We must warm our hands you say
kneeling down beside my hearth,
the hem of your skirt sweeping the floor,
your cold, white fingers raking the dying embers.
you pick them up, into your cupped palms,
carry them outside.
I must use them to start another fire,
and I will tend to it for a day;
but we need a new roof above our heads,
the wind is strong, blowing from the east.

I break twigs from trees, collect sticks
and moss; I build four walls around us,
the resin trickling down, holding them in place.
I strip the bark of a white birch,
to blend the roof into the grey sky.
There is no time for me to cover the hard ground.

You crouch on the cold ground,
murmur over the now almost black coals;
A flame leaps, rises like a tired tongue
re-kindled by a kind word.
I do not feel the cold hardness of the ground,
I have no ground under my feet.
Your lips move, uttering strange words over me,
foreign sounds I do not understand,
and I do not care,
your hands warm upon mine.

It is time for me to return the embers
to where they belong you say, rising
and you take the walls apart, stick by stick
throwing them into the fire. It flares up,
blazing wildly for a moment; suddenly
it collapses into an almost burned-out heap
as you step over it, bending down to pick
into your cupped palms lined with moss
a handful of the still glowing coals.
The wind comes, wrapping the warm ashes around you
like a grey, winged coat; he lifts you up
and you are gone.

THE POEMS YOU WRITE FOR ME

I wonder
how would it feel
if instead you would touch
my cheek and say: I do not know how
to write poems
let my hands speak for me

THERE IS NO PLACE HERE
FOR US TO LOVE

There is no place in this city
for us. Our houses are no more
a refuge. They are only walls,
mute and pale, closing us in,
white-washing our silences at night,
but not our dreams. They go on
and on outside, searching, looking
always looking. Nights turn into days.
There is no place in this city
for dreams. Not enough tall trees
to hide our shadows. Not enough
green to hope. How to fly away
when the skies are low, so very low
above, coming down on you and me?
There is no room for our breaths
here to mingle, to hear without
hearing. To touch without touching

AND OTHER INCIDENTALS

We agree. While she is away, I am
to look after the plants and other
incidentals. I water them, (with more
care than mine) each time snip off
another leaf, another frond unwilling
to unfurl. I sit at her desk, the green
top indented from the writing of her
poems; there is no use tracing them,
or writing my own, the nib of my pen
is not right for either one.
The bed looks so large, so forlorn,
no one to rest on it, no one to make love.

After, when it is over, I wash the traces
off my body in her bath with a green
soap, the scent of it unfamiliar as the place
where the mirror has been hung;

as the eyes in it, staring back at me.
Unfamiliar as the eyes back in the room,
staring at the ceiling.

THE GAME WE PLAY,
THE SAME AS LAST

(After a Welsh form)

It is as if the day came
through sunfilled doors, the same
as last. Dust is gold, a game

you play, untwisting shadows
of thin ragged haloes
inside my eyes. Pain mellows,

light laces my eyelashes, not
afraid to shatter rainbows I caught.
Again, we play games, lies we bought.

Soon, too soon, the door closes. Night
whispers: "dream now till morrow's light."
Play on shadows, spirits, blithe.

I AM YOUR DAUGHTER, MOTHER AND LOVER

Deliberately I put the wrong
key into the wrong door hoping
you will not recognize my face
and let me in. *I am your mother*
I will say, *I bring you flowers*
for your window sill. I picked them
from the garden next to yours.
They grow brighter behind high fences.
Tomorrow, I shall come back to be
your daughter. It is not everyday
I can feel innocent for being guilty.
And as you close your doors, draw
blinds over your windows and eyes,
I will whisper to you as I leave:
think kindly of me: forgive me my lover.
I came through the wrong door, I used
the wrong key.

THE BLESSED ICON

Oh you witch, you took my heart out
chopped it into pieces, nailed it
to the stone fireplace.   Now you sit and rock
combing your hair, tying golden knots
into the combed-out strands.
Swoosh   they go up the chimney, stirring up the sparks
and the fire is burning
the fire is burning.
The hair floats back; through the padlocked doors,
through the window cracks   they twist
and bend, weaving a golden chain around my neck.
Snap   go your fingers
with the half-moon nails   and they
take off the icon nailed to the stone
fireplace and suspend it from the chain
inside my hollowed-out chest.
Blessed be   blessed be
you rock, chanting sweetly, combing your hair;
your skin is aglow, amber and red
my tongue is a flame
swish   you throw a black fishnet
over my body   your thighs are fins
stretching and moving,
black fish dart into my mouth,
swim into my eye sockets
and I am caught
and I am caught.
Oh you witch, you took my heart out
chopped into pieces, nailed it
to my stony hearth.

THE MOVEMENT OF STONES

for Herbert Siebner

I am the woman with the chiselled, squared-off
shoulders, to carry the load of being in love,
of being loved.
My Lovers, you have suspended my breasts,
from your other skies. And they swing and move
like heavy stones above my head, held by you
on a hair-fine thread.

    "I want to entice, I want to be touched" the one breast pleads
    "I want to smother, I want to crush" the other cries
    "I am the sun, I am the moon
    I will decide what must be done" they chant in unison,
swaying, hitting against each other,
cracking here and there.
    "Have I no say in what I want to do? after all,
    I am the rightful owner of both of you" I say to them
    "being in love, being loved,
    you have forfeited all your rights!" the breasts exclaim,
joyfully swinging, hitting one another,
cracking a bit more.
    "No say,
    no say at all,
    but oh, what fun we both have
    we can do as we like!" they sing loudly,
swaying to and fro
    "But you are not.
    You are told what you want,
    what to feel, you are stones! Listen to the crumbling,
    breaking, you are falling into pieces,
    burying my feet!"

BUT GLASS IS LIKE CONCRETE, IT WILL NOT BREAK

Suspended high above crossed
streets, behind thick glass
walls, I sit, watch you be-
low me standing. You do not fit
into my eye. Street lights
dim, swallow you whole. So be it.
For there is no more room left
on the concrete for shadows to
lengthen, no room to spread.
Concrete is hard like glass.
I would put my fist through
it and watch the splinters fall.
It would be easier then for
me to breathe, knowing that even
the light shadows that disappear
have tender feet.
But my hands are gloved, smooth in white
kid, leather thin, so very thin

I WANT TO VISIT IF I MAY

There are 77 steps leading to wherever
she lives. No use me knocking
at the other doors I see along the way,
the time is mostly holidays. "Out
for coffee", "Will open at a later time",
"Be back, please call again." I read
these signs, climbing up and up the oak-
dark stairs, the musty smell of hallways
rising to my nostrils.
I rest on each landing, peer through
the small leaded panes, the glass
blinded with cobwebs and dust.
It must be long ago anyone wanted
to see what is outside.

Before me is a wall of frosted glass,
a door knob framed into a door. I try
to open it without disturbing the quiet.
It swings back into a huge room.
I measure the distance from ceiling
to floor, its height lowered by spiders,
each one suspended from a single thread.

It is still too high for the head
of the woman who is pacing the floor.
"How do you do" I murmur politely,
(the lofty ceiling makes it sound
so formal) recognizing my best friend's
black hair. "I want to visit with you
if I may."
"I am busy now. I have begun writing
a poem about you, you must excuse me
until I'm finished. But do sit down
in this corner here, which the sun fills
every time or so. My thoughts will flow
easier that way."

It is now two or three years that I have
been sitting here, she is still pacing
and writing the poem, but I do not mind.
At least I have a place where I can rest,
after having climbed these steps
to wherever she lives.

AND THERE ARE THOSE
WHO KEEP ME COMPANY

I must confess, it took me
three years to unknot the cobwebs
in my present home. Though I admit
many of them were quite old,
were never unpacked, just stored
helter-skelter in wicker baskets
and trunks up in the attic.

With great care, I wound them
into huge balls, lucky me
each one as light as a feather.
All winter I pored over books
and books on knitting. Only now
I have begun to knit stockings
and socks. I hope to progress,
make a long, narrow muffler.

At times I do get tired counting
stitches, holding needles, I go
outside, into the garden to poke
them into the dirt, but they make
holes and I fill them with bulbs
of hyacinths, snowdrops and crocuses.

Once every Friday or so,
I invite my friends to tea,
sit them comfortably in my lawn
chairs, ask them to please note
the freshly dug-up soil, I promise
them, soon a garden full of spring
flowers. They usually accept
my generosity, assure me, while
warming their hands on the hot
glasses, that 'yes, thank you kindly,
it's very good of you to think
of us while you are so busy.'

I offer each one of them a pair
of stockings (or socks, if they
prefer) hesitantly, I mention
the muffler.
"I might not be able to knit one,
but I will try my best" I assure
them in turn, between one lump
of sugar and turning a heel
of a red and green striped stocking.
But they do not seem to mind,
their faces rosy from the brisk wind.

"You are a true friend" they murmur,
wiping daintly their mouths,
"it's such a pleasure to be with you,
such welcome change from whatever
else we would be doing. But do tell
us, of course if it does not
interfere with the counting of
the stitches, what do you plan to do
after you have used up all
the cobweb yarn?"
"O my dears" I reply, inserting
the needle to secure a loop,
"the true work is still ahead of me."

AMICUS CERTUS IN
RE INCERTA CERNITUR

These are my friends; their faces
veiled with muted grey to be kind
for the sake of my memories. To be
kind even more, they are wearing
clothes of once or so ago.

I want to put my arms around them,
pretend that I do see the purple
silk, the gossamer shawls, even
the pearls strung around their necks,
glowing softly with their skin.
But I am afraid. They look so fragile.
If I should touch them, they might
turn into beads and fall like tears
down their pale cheeks, their pale
bossoms. I am afraid of the clatter.

All this is in your honour I read
through the grey, its hue uncertain
as the eyes they lower. They are kind
to me, do not want me to see in them
my own reflection. *You are starting*
a new life I hear them count the beads,
touch each knot inbetween. *How very good*
of you. We shall then not see you for
a while. But do take with you the blue
jug which never belonged to you, now
that you are leaving behind the corner
in which it stood.

AND THERE ARE THOSE
WHO WEAR SILK AT NIGHT

There is this man who walks
each day of the year the streets
of different cities.

Miss he said,
stopping me on a corner of a town,
bordering on something bigger
than that, correcting himself,
as I turned around:
Madam, I have a shoebox full
of silkworms which I give away
one at a time. But today I have
more than I care to count.
Would you like to have them all?

I thanked the man, took the box
(not a bootsize but a standard)
and swaying with the squirming worms
inside it, I came home. I put
them in a corner free of draught,
and begun to sweep all my clothes
out of the closets, into a green
garbage bag, leaving only one dress,
which is pure silk. I sat at
my desk with a pad and a pen.

Dear Man, this is a letter.
Please do not come to see me
from now on. Lately my skin
does not feel like silk when you
touch me. Starting today, I shall
be raising my own silkworms.
Do remember me though kindly,
since I have written this
in red ink.
P.S. If anything should change
in the state of my mind, I will
let you know thereafter.
> *With all my previous affection*
> *here is my signature.*

I carried the silkworms into
the bedroom, deposited them on
the bed, which of late has
become much larger than I thought.
Please consider half of it
your home I told the worms,
I will line your side with mulberry
branches for your comfort. My only
interference: I might pick a berry
and eat it everytime or so.
Other than that, you are free
to spin. I myself, will be satisfied
with the two feather pillows.

It's been now over a year, (a year
and a half, to be exact) since
the worms and I began sharing
the bed. Each morning we greet
each other between the fretwork
of the mulberry leaves and my
punched-down pillows, exchanging
pleasantries:
How was your night? How is
the spinning of silk progressing?
Ah that's wonderful. O   sorry
to hear that; o well, tomorrow
surely will be much better.

Every fourth Saturday morning
I bring them eggs, sunny-side-up,
prepared with special care when
the day is rainy. They thrive
on the diet, enjoying the service.
In return, on alternate weekends,
they deposit six cocoons on my
night table.
Soon I will have enough to plan
a new wardrobe. I have not thought
about The Dear Man except on
nights when the moon is full,
and I tend to get restless.
My hunger is satisfied, my lips
a perpetual mulberry colour,
a sweet taste in my mouth.

NARWHAL MY PALE NEW LOVER

This morning I did not miss you.
My thighs are still warm from rubbing
against the white flanks of my new lover.
(If you look at me, you will see
my cheeks aglow with true colour.)
The bruises you have left upon my
right breast faded away,
I needed not to explain them.
He nuzzled the pale of my skin,
nibbling here and there; his
two canines grew larger, larger
twisting into one hard tusk; soon
he was thrusting it deeper, deeper
exploring my most tender spots.
Be careful of my other lover's dreams
I told him, *his hands keep folding,*
unfolding me like a leaf,
tracing my scars with knowing fingers,
and he loves me best with his eyes closed.

I am your new lover he replied
"Lo now, my strength is in my loins,
my force in the navel of my belly.
Do not be afraid. I will love
you with the passion of a lion;
I will carry you, riding high
upon my back with the swiftness
of a deer into the deepest
of deep fabulous sea. The salt shall
be kind to your age-marred wounds."

THERE IS THIS MAN

There is this man who wears clothes
I do not know where they were bought.
I do not know the brand of his shoes,
(though I remember their colours).
I am not sure of his eating habits
at breakfast. And sometimes I wonder
on which side of the bed he sleeps,
what kind of pillow he prefers;
and it seems I never have the time
to ask. But he is the man who
perforates the straps of my shoes
so I can walk, and whose handkerchief
I often find inside my purse.

THAT'S ONE THING
HE WON'T KNOW

When he saw her again, it was
in his easier life. The curious
void inside his chest, felt like
a silent house, empty of creaking.
Not that he ever counted his
heart beat. It was just there.
Good he said to himself,
*now I have peace. I will use
the space for other things,
watch it from within* He planted
three different seeds, did not
bother to find out, where they
came from. *I shall water them whenever
I like; other than that, they must
fend for themselves.* And he went on
with his easier life. Once or twice
he felt a stir, a movement looked
inside himself, poured some water
and that was that. Another time,
his eye became itchy, he rubbed it,
felt a twig pushing through it,
took the scissors, trimmed it neatly.
The next time, he noticed a flower
growing out of his ear, looked at it,
liked its size, left it there.
When he saw her again, she was
sitting on a cloud, looking sweet
and innocent. *Look* he called
up to her, *I feel good about you;
the empty space you have left, is now
fertile with other things. I
planted three seeds, what they were,
I don't know. But one is growing
into a tree, the other is a flower,
the third seed did not come up.
Tell me, have you by any chance
kept room inside me for yourself?*

72

THE MAN WITH THE STOLEN EYES

The man walking beside me pushes
a large fish ahead of him. Its
great body, of a curious kind
slithers on the pavement, the man's
spliced fingers hold the twitching
tail firmly.

Madam he says, his other hand saluting,
I was looking for you this morning
and the morning before. I have this
urge to ask you to be my mistress.
Though first, we must establish
our future relationship on solid
grounds. Tomorrow you will be busy
eating fish and I must eat it
the day thereafter. The problem is,
I cannot light a fire or do
a thing on the Sabbath. Would that
interfere with your faith?

Not necessarily I answer, *my mother,*
a Russian Orthodox, crossed us,
her three children, 3 times in the morning,
then again, at night. My father
insisted only that we were confirmed
at fourteen, he being a mild
Protestant. One of my brothers is
a convert. The other, up north keeps
the souls and bodies of Lutherans
from freezing. As for myself,
I say The Rosary each night,
make the Sign of the Cross passing
a church, be it Russian Orthodox,
Protestant or a Synagogue. The only
thing worrying me is, I am also
superstitious — a man with black hair
pushing a fish ahead of him?

73

No matter the man says, *just consider*
my offer. You see, they stole
my eyes for someone else, and instead
of a white cane I am pushing
this fish. But lucky for me, they left
my other senses intact. And my sense
of smell is telling me you are right
for me. This is what I propose:
since we both have to eat fish
(you on Friday, and I the day thereafter)
do come, live with me. I will keep
the fire going 'til Friday, then you'll
chop off a piece of this fish
for your dinner, (it will not matter,
the fish is quite large). The next day,
you take over and cook another chunk
for me in a broth with carrots,
parsley and onions. (O yes, don't
forget the almonds.) After, just light
my seven-arm candelabrum, sit by me
and watch me eat the Sabbath meal.
The rest will take care of itself
for I am a loving person under my skin.
(Some say I am a self-confessed
misanthrope, but that's just a mis-
quoted line.) I have touched your
sleeve and know there is more
underneath it. I want to write
about you in braille.

All is well, as he said. He keeps
the fire going until Friday,
I take over when the clock
strikes midnight. We go for walks,
hand in hand, with the other
hand he pushes what is left of the fish,
its backbone and tail (the head
I cooked last Sabbath) the fish
guiding us now quite docile.
He reads to me, touching my knuckles
affectionately as they flex,
respond to his poetry.

IV

THE THREE

Open up, we brought wings for you   L.K.

AUCTIONING OFF EYES

for Sylvia Skelton

I am putting up for auction my reality,
I will accept the lowest bid.
Now, almost totally blind, I must
learn to survive on instinct and smell.
I will give away the two loaves I have
and steal a lily, learn how to touch
colour and fragrance.

EHECATL, THE LORD
OF THE WINDS

"Lord of the Winds, oh Whistling Toad,
we build for you a round temple,
no corners. Precious Lord, put on
your mask, breath into us new life
and make us, your cradle, fertile."

I am the Lord of the Morning Star,
Of Hope and all the things beautiful.

"Lord of the Winds, oh Whistling Toad,
bring down the heaven. The golden
rain of spring, the sacred blue of
summer. Give us the red rain with
ripening fruit of our harvest."

I am the Lord of the Morning Star,
each dawn I rise from the serpent's mouth.

And as he spoke, he saw through the walls
of his temple the young moon goddess
within waters, opening to him
her vulva like a thirsty flower.
He broke the walls, swept toward her,
the shape of his desire a column
of hard lava, and he breathed into her
the fertile breath of life. In good time
she brought forth conch shells to call him father.

"Let us rejoice!" we cry, "we will gather
your children like wind-jewels, wear them
around our necks. Oh Lord, they are holy, holy!"

MY NEW WAX FINGERTIPS

Between here and there is a tongue
on which I try to soothe my fingers.
The first time I came near it, lying
peacefully on a sunny window sill.
I put my hand upon it, it shrivelled
into a tight knot and disappeared
for many days.

When I saw it again, it was dozing
by a hearth. This time I did
not touch it, I only asked:
*My mother and father lost me
a long time ago; can you tell me
where I can be found?* The tongue
came forward, curling, uncurling
timidly, suddenly it leaped
stabbing my hand with pronged flames,
scorching my fingertips black. *I am
the sister you never had* it hissed,
next time you wake me, be careful!
It retreated, burying itself in ashes.

I melted all the candles in the house,
dribbling the hot wax over my fingers
to cover the black; I went to a pond
full of swans, to harden and mold
my new fingertips in the cold
water. I picked a tightly closed bud
from a near-by bush, it crushed,
oozing tacky, honey-like liquid,
staining my pale fingertips.

I held it out to a stranger,
feeding the birds with breadcrumbs.
Can you tell me what the green
tastes like? I asked.
I thought I saw his eyes darken
I thought I saw his lips turn black.

Behind the trees two children are
rocking on horses in the playground.
Your horses must be hungry I called out
and the three of us collected hands full
of pebbles and fed them. *Look, they are*
licking your fingertips! The girl exclaimed.
It feels good I said, gave them a few
more stones. *They've had enough to eat*
the children said, *now you come*
and ride with us giddy-up giddy-up
they cried, mounting the wooden horses,
clicking their tongues.

AND THE CURDLED MILK
RUNNETH SWEET AGAIN

Before they were weaned, three
of her children died. On the first
nothing day, after her seventh child
was born she got up at dawn, spread
out her finery on the bed, lay beside
it, and died.

They dressed her in her best, slaughtered
a red dog for company. In three days
she was gone in a cloud of smoke and set
out upon her journey, with the creature
hobbling beside her, still dripping blood.
They travelled west, to where the seeds
push through from below. On the way
they saw a passage through two giant rocks,
the dog limping ahead. "I must follow
the scent" she thought, hurrying behind him.
As she passed between them, a terrible wind
arose, swaying, moving the rocks. They clashed
together, she barely reached the other side,
her hem caught, her garments torn off.
Clutching close her long black hair to cover
her nakedness, she followed the dog's blood-
dripping trail, along a mountain ridge,
three-toe-wide. She kept her eyes away
from the precipice, looking inwards into
memories. "Soon I will see my babies,
cradled in the branches of the Milk Tree,
suckling on nippled fruit; I will kiss
and caress their downy heads, watch the milky
nectar trickle down their chins. And may sorrow
be gentle to my breasts, swollen with
curdled milk.

I will walk up still another road, to visit
my brother. A happy child he was, drowning
in sweet water, the giver of all that is
alive. I will watch him frolic among
the golden haze of pollen and maize, between
the prisms of a soft rain. When I am through
the wind of knives, my flesh whittled away
by blades, I will come back, lay seven aramanth
seeds at the feet of Lady Precious Green,
and ask her for a pair of wings.
Then I will return to my house, to sit
upon a nosegay of fresh flowers,
and tantalize the nostrils of my man."

FOREST FULL OF RAIN

I *THE WINGED WOMAN*

I shall speak of wondrous wings,
fabulous feathers, a magic story
of a man in love.

It all began simply enough.
He caught a glimpse of her
with his other eye, many years ago.
He dreamed of her, for as long
as a dream could last. In torment,
he began to search for her
when the sun was out. When he found her,
she smiled at him and said: *come*
back when the time is right.   In time
he came back, she looked deep into
his eyes, touched his lids with
a feather, and was gone in a flurry
of sun-speckled cloud. Again he searched
and searched. He found her, sleeping
peacefully in a forest full of rain.
Weakened by desire, he made love to her,
but she did not wake. And he brought gifts
to lay at her feet, gifts befitting
the richest of kings: an enchanted
jade frog, a fat ebony Buddha with a diamond
belly button and a female piglet
swathed in ostrich plumes. "I have
given her all I have" he said to himself,
"my other eye, my dreams and all the riches
I possess, now she must learn to love me."

She woke and rose with sleep still deep
in her eyes, her feet carrying her
toward a cliff, and she was singing
the song no man ever could resist.
He followed her to the edge
stretching out his arms, he touched her,
saw wings growing from her shoulder
blades, wings of fabulous feathers,
red and gold. She smiled at him,
her eyes still closed, she brushed
his cheek with her wings and flew away,
grey early mist rising from the sea.

II *THE BIRTH OF THE SEIRĒN*

The mist spreads its grey. The waters,
the skies are still. Such stillness
can pierce the ears of all creatures.

A ripple, a splash; a wave sighs
like a child in sleep. Hush.   The earth
is a still cradle, will shatter
with the thinnest of breath

A spray rises; a fan of feathers
opens the sky, shatters the air like glass.
A ripple. A wave. A fishtail arches
out of the deep. Can you hear the song
no man ever could resist? Will she
steal the living to share her fate?

III *HIS GODMOTHERS GIFT,*
THE SILVER SPOON

He took off the silver spoon
from the chain around his neck,
he began to hollow out the sea.
Spoon by spoon he carried the water
to the valley, his hands becoming
whiter and whiter, encrusted in salt.
No one knows how many times he made
the journey except perhaps the path,
worn thin by his feet. Weary,
he fell asleep between two rocks
hugging the shore. The spoon moved
across the sand, picked up a
snake-skin drying on the rock
stretched it over a mast and sailed
toward the open sea. Afraid of losing it,
he began to swim. Ahead, he saw
a huge rock, jutting out, his love there
plaiting seaweed in her hair. Again
she smiled at him. Unable to resist
her dazzling smile, he climbed the rock,
to sit beside her. She took his
salt-encrusted hands into her own
and said: *the time is right.*
The salt brittled away, leaving his hands
smooth once more. She placed a tiny fish
into his palm and said: *When the sun
comes down, follow the fish.*

And she sang to him, until the last
sunrays set the grey cliff aflame.
The fish jumped from his hand,
disappeared into the deep. He rubbed
his eyes, saw his love's golden hair
entangled in a fishtail, shimmering
emerald-green, sapphire-blue, cutting
through the waters. He touched his chest,
could not feel his heart beat.

If you want, I will show you the rock
on which they sat. Only it must be
the first night of a full moon.
You will see her take the moonbeams
laced into her hair and light two candles
in her lover's eyes. But only those
who are in love will see the candles burn.

I AM TO BE
THE NEW CHATELAINE

Three came, stood in my doorway
with their faces painted white,
their eyes circled black. Each took
a flower off his hat, giving it
to me. Their red-slashed mouths
said, uttering no sound: *take out
your stained glass windows, their colours
are frightening the spring away!
I cannot.* I answered, turning around
for them to read my lips. *I am to be
the new chatelaine in another man's
manor. I am embroidering a silk dress
just like the one that I am wearing now
and I must follow the pattern.
But I lost my thimble, the needle
is pricking my fingertips, staining
the silk red.* I showed them the cloth.
*We shall then stay here and watch you
keep the colours true.* The mouths spoke
without a sound.

They sat down, encircling me
with their black eyes, and began
to unwind my spools of silk thread,
stretching it between their fingers.
Here is the blue which you will need;
one of the mouths said, biting off
three elbow lengths. *Here is the green
which you don't want, but you will
take,* the other one said, holding up
his little finger, the thread wound
tightly around it. *I will watch
the pattern emerge from below,*

the third one said, lying down
under the embroidery hoop, and he
tossed a spool. It bounced over
the threshold, the red thread
unravelling down the careful lawns,
toward the woods, edging the gardens.
Bring it back, I must have them all!
I cried. *Ah, that's where the other
manor is, just a spool's-throw away,
all moss-covered brick, turrets
hollow-eyed. Tell your needle to be
quicker!* his eyes poked at me.
*I cannot go there, I must wait
until the servants all arrive, light
the candles, sweep the cobwebs,
trim the vines from the floors. Bring
my spool back, this is one colour
that I must have!* He just lay there,
watching my needle dart in and out.

I just wished your roof away, he remarked
with soul-quiet eyes. *All that light
is blinding me, how will I finish
my work?* I exclaimed, the embroidery
falling to the ground.
*I must finish my embroidery.
But I am missing one spool of silk,
and my roof has disappeared,
and the servants are yet to come.
Oh that light!
Oh that light! Until to-morrow
I must close, rest my eyes.*

THEY READIED THE HOUSE
BEFORE I WOKE

Before I had time to plump
the last cushion, The Three
told me I had sold this house.
The rats that live underneath
are cutting through the rock
it stands on. They thrive on
the poison you have left in all
the dark corners; soon the saltspray
from the sea will blind all your
windowpanes, the gale will shut all
the doors and there will be no other
corners left.

I took everything precious to me,
put them into the breastpocket
of my red silk shirt, wound three
strings from my guitar around my
arm and followed them to see
the new house I had bought. It stood
surrounded by washing blowing in the wind
suspended from empty windowframes
buried in rubble. Hills of loose dirt,
pinned by junipers and dwarf pines.
Inside were five bedrooms, with flowers
painted on the walls and beds, the
colour of an angry sky before a storm.
The man that used to live here left
you these two grand pianos to fill
the void of creaking your other steps
had, The Three said, showing me
the drawing rooms. Pressing my arm
against my pocket to keep my guitar
strings from tinkling, I followed
The Three through a long corridor.

This is the sunniest place in this
house, they said, opening the door
to a room sparkling with mosaic walls.
You can sit here each morning and noon,
even at night if you want.
In the middle was a leaf-shaped pool,
white marble, veined blue, and it was
boiling with bodies of huge salamanders,
baby cotton-mouths, eels slithering
in spermy water. *They are here*
to amuse you on rainy days, they said,
and left. A head rose out of the pool
a slime-covered creature, it followed
me as I ran to the door. I caught its
head between the crack, squeezed it,
trying to pull the door shut. It scraped
my leg with sharp teeth, forcing the door
open; suddenly it purred, rubbing
its flanks against me, its green
slit-eyes looking demurely into my
still pupils. *It is here to protect your*
treasures, I Heard The Three say, closing
the door of my new house behind them.

THE STRAWBERRY PLATE AND I

Part I

The night before (or was it
the night before that?) The Three came,
shook the cowbells above my door
and said: *"Let us in. We brought wings*
for you. We collected the feathers
from here to there, lost only three
somewhere in between."
"My bird is still asleep. Last night
he was feeding me strawberries off
a china plate, and his beak got tired,"
I called out, padlocking the door.
"Let us in. The hinges on your door
are rusty, and they will give in
if we only breathe," they said,
shaking the cowbells harder.
I took a spider off a wall to spin
a web to sturdy the door.
Spinne am Morgen bringt Kummer und Sorgen;
Spinne am Mittag bringt Glück am Drittag;
Spinne am Abend bringt Freude und Laben;
I sang, walking back and forth,
watching the spider weave. *"Why are you*
singing in German? Are you frightened?"
They called through the keyhole, disturbing
the web.

Spinne am Morgen
Spinne am Mittag
Spinne am Abend I sang louder, louder
ignoring the torn web. *"Open up.*
Take these wings. Three feathers are
missing, and it might be hard to fly
but it's worth a try!" They shouted,
scraping the door. *"My bird is still asleep,"*
I told them again, tiptoed into my
Wintergarten, opened the cage. I took out
the sleeping bird, carried him
to the door and I pushed him through
the keyhole into their mouths to stop
them from shouting.
"Now I can finish eating the strawberries,"
I said to myself, going back to the bird-
cage, closing its door quietly behind me.

Part II

IF ONLY I COULD BE SNOWHITE

"She finished eating her strawberries,"
The Three said, peeking through the plants,
their eyelashes raking the fronds.
"Now she is looking into the bird bath
to see how red her lips have become.
Hello," they called, *"are you satisfied*
with the berries and the colour of your
lips?" "Go away," I told them, reaching
for the swinging bird trapeze. *"Go swing*
outside, to put colour on your cheeks,"
they breathed through the hanging plants,
making them sway. *"Go away,"* I told them
again, *"the tree is too old to hold me up,*
you are wishing me ill!" I swung higher,
higher, my hair tangling up between
the cage's slats. *"Let us help you,"*
The Three said, advancing through the flower
pots. *"It's a jungle if you ask me, you can*
hardly see the sun," one of them remarked,
taking one pot after another, heaving it
through the windows. *"Get out!"* I cried,
"Just loosen my hair, before you go."
"Not until you promise to go outside,"

they said, running their fingers through
the tangled strands. *"Nice colour, nice
texture,"* they smacked their lips, rubbing
their cheeks against my hair. *"I wish
it was black, now that my lips are red,
my skin is already white, then I could be
Snowhite. And I could pretend, that you are
the three, left-over dwarfs."* I said, trying
to look into their eyes. *"You can be what you
want to be, just stop moving, tearing at
your hair, and get out from the bird cage!"*
they said, holding on to the strands.
*"If I do what you say, and become what I want,
what will I do swinging from a tree branch
with the horse and the Prince waiting
down below?"* I asked, squirming.
*"You can teach them both to eat strawberries
from a swinging china plate."*

MY OTHER FACE

I *THE WAITING*

"Stop looking at me; first I must
collect the fragments of my other face.
The duck, that just flew over me
descending on the pond, broke it
with her wings. But if you stand
above it on these rocks you can stop
the water from falling with your hands,
and scattering the pieces." I tell The Three.
It's too high for us to climb; besides,
we buried our hands in our pockets."
They call, and I could feel their eyes
probe my cautious, bent spine, I could see
their reflection in the water, their bodies
coming together, coming apart. I could
hear the scuffling of their feet
on the gravel path, tiny pebbles rolled
toward me, wrapped in fallen petals
of hibiscus trees. *"Stop kicking!"* I call out,
"You are disturbing the water! How will I
find my other face now that I have forgotten
what colour my eyes were when I spoke?"
"That's true," they say *"your mouth always*
had trouble saying the same things as your
eyes. Nor did your skin fit properly
over your bones."

"*That is the fault of my cheeks,
their planes are always confusing me.*"
I answer, poking furtively with a stick
in the water. I lift out a petal, pressing it
against my nose. It feels like skin,
but has no fragrance. How strange.
"*Look over there,*" I tell The Three,
"*at those two, sitting on the bench,
they must be lovers, holding hands
like that. He is stroking her cheek,
telling her her skin smells like spring,
she reminds me of someone,   oh yes —
I must go to her and ask, why are you
wearing my face?*"
The Three are watching my stick push
petals together, apart. The breeze
carries the woman's voice; "*yes, we do
have three days*" she is saying, closing
her eyes. I see them walk away,
disappear down the path. I think I will
wait for her here and ask her,
"*what did I do in those three days?*"

II *THE SEARCH FOR BONES*

It is now 3 times 3 days (or is it
3 times 3 years?) I am sitting at the edge
of the pond. Even The Three have disappeared.
My stick lies broken by my side, it is my hands
now, cold, trying to push apart the clouds,
darkening the water. I peer into the pond,
although my skin is gone, I want to see
my bones. But my eyes will not obey.
They dart about, chameleons on the fallen
petals, weighing down the clouds. Suddenly
my fingers enmesh them, they stare at me
immobile. *"What lies are you going to feed me
this time?"* I ask, tightening my grip
to make them flinch. *"Who wants to know
you or your mouth, what tongue do you want
us to speak?"* Before I know, they slither out.
I think, I must stay here until the pond
is dry, to find the bones of my other face.
Bones always remain the same.

NOTES

DO NOT OPEN THE SEA INTO MY HOUSE

This poem is based on one of the oldest and most sacred Polish traditions, the honouring and greeting of a guest entering a home. I will quote two proverbs which will perhaps convey the feeling of the people. *Gosc w dom — Bog w dom* (guest in the house — God in the house), *Czym chata bogata — tym rada* (whatever riches in this cottage — are yours with gladness). The ritual of greeting on the threshold I describe in this poem, is still practised in many parts of Poland.

NARWHAL MY PALE NEW LOVER

The second and third lines of the second part of the poem are a quotation from *The Hebrew Book of Guidance* by D. D. Rimes.

THE MOVEMENT OF STONES

This poem was written in response to a woodcut by Herbert Siebner with the title, *"About to move itself, bending find the burden of the lust."*

EHECATL

Ehecatl is the Lord of the Winds in Aztec mythology. He was also referred to as The Whistling Toad and Lord of the Morning Star.

AND THE CURDLED MILK RUNNETH SWEET AGAIN

This poem is based on the Aztec after-life mythology. The underworld was divided into four abodes to which the dead humans travelled: the Mictlan for those who died of natural causes, the Tlalocan, home of the rain god Tlaloc and his consort Chalchihuitlicue, Lady Precious Green, for those who died by drowning or diseases associated with water (this was one of the most desirable places with lush vegetation, flowers, butterflies and rain), the Heaven of the Milk Tree for babies who died before they were weaned, and the fourth place which was the highest heaven and reserved for those who gave their lives for their nation and also for women who died in giving birth.